T0356428

The Campus History Series

COLLEGE OF THE OZARKS

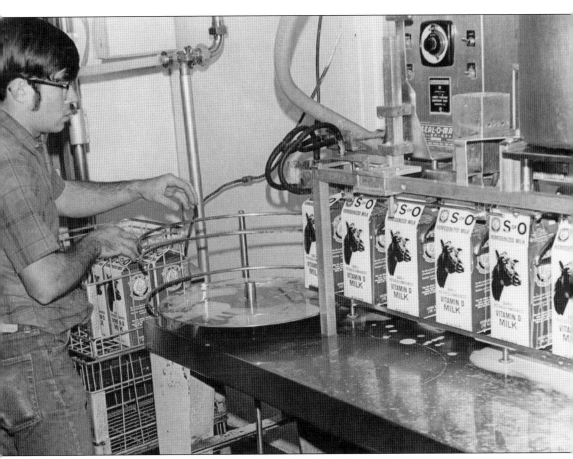

FILLING MILK CARTONS. Milk from the college's dairy is used in the cafeteria, restaurant, and ice cream shop. During the 1960s, these half-gallon cartons featured images of a cow and the college seal and noted that the milk was homogenized. Students then and now are involved in every aspect of running the dairy. (Courtesy College of the Ozarks archival collection.)

ON THE FRONT COVER: LAKE HONOR. Lake Honor is centrally located on campus and provides a place to enjoy conversation or a picnic. Prior to the lake's construction in 1931, this area was a lot for livestock. Lake Honor's name was suggested by benefactor L.W. Hyer. He created an eponymous award as a way to recognize students who excelled academically and who received no demerits for misconduct. (Courtesy College of the Ozarks archival collection.)

COVER BACKGROUND: MAINE CLUBHOUSE. Dobyns Hall was the first building at Point Lookout. This postcard shows the building when it was still named Maine Clubhouse, used by a hunting and fishing club. (Courtesy College of the Ozarks archival collection.)

The Campus History Series

COLLEGE OF THE OZARKS

Gwen Simmons

ARCADIA
PUBLISHING

Published by Arcadia Publishing
Charleston, South Carolina

Printed in the United States of America

Library of Congress Control Number: 2024938204

For all general information, please contact Arcadia Publishing:
Telephone 843-853-2070
Fax 843-853-0044
E-mail sales@arcadiapublishing.com

Visit us on the Internet at www.arcadiapublishing.com

To my family and to all whose lives have been changed at Point Lookout

CONTENTS

ACKNOWLEDGMENTS

Anyone wanting to know more about the College of the Ozarks owes a debt of gratitude to Townsend Godsey. Townsend and his wife, Helen, published *The Flight of the Phoenix* in 1984. The book documents the history of the school and remains the best source of information about that history. I also want to recognize Bob Good. His unpublished manuscript about his parents, Robert M. and Lyta Davis Good, provided valuable details about the school.

I appreciate the help of alumni director Angela Williamson, museum director Annette Sain, and retired archivist Laura Lane. All three helped with photographs and advice. The public relations department helped with recent photographs, as did Karen Terry at the College Press. Thanks also to the college administrators who supported the project from the proposal stage.

Unless otherwise noted, all images are courtesy of the archival collections at College of the Ozarks.

INTRODUCTION

Perched on a bluff overlooking Lake Taneycomo near Branson, Missouri, sits the College of the Ozarks. The sprawling 1,000-acre campus is home to a unique institution. Students do not pay tuition. Instead, all full-time students work at a campus job to help cover the cost of their education. It is an educational model that has worked for over a century.

What is now the College of the Ozarks had its origins in a desire to help students from the Ozarks who did not have the means to pay for an education. The then School of the Ozarks was founded in 1906 at a time when public education was not easily accessible in the Missouri Ozarks. Taney County, where the college is located, had no public high schools at the time. Poverty, poor roads, and a lack of transportation made it difficult for children to go to school. Presbyterian missionary James Forsythe recognized that a different educational opportunity was needed. He wrote multiple letters to the Missouri Synod of the Presbyterian Church asking for financial support to establish a school. As Forsythe put it, "The primary object of such a school should be to offer the best intellectual training under the best possible moral and Christian auspices . . . The aim should be to make the school a self-sustaining 'family' by requiring all students to spend a portion of their time in the various duties assigned them."

While a positive answer did not come immediately, it did come. Articles of incorporation were drawn up and the School of the Ozarks ("S of O") was granted a charter by the State of Missouri on November 19, 1906. By September 24, 1907, S of O was ready for its opening and dedication, with the local newspaper inviting everyone to a fish fry to celebrate. The agenda for the day included enrolling students in primary, intermediate, and high school classes. Music and speeches from dignitaries were also included in the program.

The first years of the school's existence were not easy. Money was always tight. Finding administrators and teachers willing to work in the Ozarks for small salaries was a challenge. A nearly final blow struck when a fire destroyed the building at the school's original site in Forsyth, Missouri. But there was a silver lining in the clouds. The insurance settlement from the fire was just enough to buy a building and property across the county near Branson and Hollister. In the fall of 1915, the School of the Ozarks reopened as a high school at what would become Point Lookout. The mission of the school remained the same, "to provide the advantages of a Christian education for the youth of both sexes, especially those found worthy, but who are without sufficient means to procure such training."

Hard times continued at Point Lookout, but the arrival of Dr. Robert M. Good as president in 1921 set the stage for the next chapters in the school's history. He always managed to find just enough money to keep the school afloat even during the Great Depression. He also managed to find space for those students who were desperate for an education and willing to work at any job to get it. One advantage to the school's rural location at the new campus was that there was room to grow crops, raise animals, and be self-sufficient. Students from the Ozarks were often experienced at those agricultural chores and took on much of the work at the school's farms. Other students learned new skills in construction, cooking, or secretarial work.

As the years passed, enrollment grew as did the physical plant on campus. Dr. M. Graham Clark became president in 1952 when Good retired. One of Clark's priorities was building Williams Memorial Chapel. The neo-Gothic chapel, built by students under the supervision of staff members, opened in 1958. Its architectural style and location at the center of campus make it an iconic building at the school.

Dr. Clark also led the way in planning for the school's future. By the time he became president, public high schools were available throughout the Ozarks. School leaders turned their attention to higher education, establishing a junior college in 1956. For several years, the junior college and the high school operated side by side, but the high school was eliminated in 1967 while the junior college became a four-year college. The change to higher education meant different programs of study, more staff and faculty, and more facilities. However, those students accepted to the new college were still required to work on campus. In fact, an article in the *Wall Street Journal* published in 1973 dubbed the school "Hard Work U."—a nickname that stuck.

Dr. Clark retired in 1980, and the college entered an unsettled time with many changes in leadership and looming financial problems. When Dr. Jerry Davis was hired as president in 1988, difficult decisions had to be made to keep the college solvent. A very visible change was also made during the early years of the Davis presidency when the institution's name was changed from School of the Ozarks to College of the Ozarks ("C of O").

The college's centennial in 2006 found the institution thriving and ready to celebrate. Special events included a picnic near the school's original location in Forsyth and a ball with attendees in period costumes. A time capsule was buried near the chapel. The campus museum created an exhibit of artifacts while bakers prepared a 101-pound fruitcake, an homage to a campus treat.

Now well past its centennial birthday, the College of the Ozarks is nationally recognized for its dedication to its original mission to educate those from the region who are willing to work towards their goals. The college operates with five foundational goals or pillars that recognize the academic, Christian, cultural, patriotic, and vocational aspects of C of O.

The true measure of success at College of the Ozarks is not the accolades it has been awarded, although those accolades are numerous. It is not the prominent guests or success on the athletic fields, although those have also been numerous. C of O's success comes from the lives it has changed, as students receive an education of the head, hands, and heart.

One

The Beginning

It was June 1901 when Rev. James Forsythe first arrived in the Ozarks. The recent seminary graduate had dreamed of going overseas as a missionary but instead was assigned to the Missouri Ozarks. He was a circuit rider, serving churches in Forsyth (no connection between the man and the town; note the different spellings), Sparta, and Mansfield. As he traveled the hills and valleys of his territory, Forsythe was appalled by the lack of educational opportunities. There were no public high schools nearby. Elementary schools only met for a few months each year, and teachers were often poorly trained. There was no transportation to the schools, which made it impossible for many children to attend. Reverend Forsythe wrote to his superiors in the Presbyterian Church, describing the conditions and asking for financial support to establish a residential school. It took several years, but the School of the Ozarks was officially chartered on November 19, 1906.

Work on the campus was already underway when the charter was signed. On October 17, 1906, residents of Forsyth were invited to march from the town square to the school site to lay the cornerstone of Mitchell Hall. Due to a lack of funds, it would be nearly a year before the building was ready for students. But even though money was tight, persistence paid off, and on September 24, 1907, the School of the Ozarks welcomed 128 students in grades one to eleven. Principal W.I. Utterback's staff included an assistant principal, two teachers, a matron, and a farm superintendent.

From the beginning, the School of the Ozarks had a work program where students worked in exchange for tuition. Typical chores included laundry, gardening, and cutting wood. Bible classes were also a part of daily life, with the board of trustees providing a Bible for every student. The school's values were evident from the beginning with the Latin phrase "Work with mind, hand, and spirit" in the official seal of the institution.

JAMES FORSYTHE. When Presbyterian missionary James Forsythe came to the Ozarks in 1901, he found extreme poverty and a lack of educational opportunities. One day he met a boy, Ben Cummings, out hunting. During their conversation, Cummings told Forsythe that he had graduated eighth grade and would like further education but did not have money to go away to school. Forsythe described the dire conditions in several letters to Presbytery officials, but his meeting with Cummings produced another eloquent letter. In it, Forsythe proposed a school for "boys and girls who are deserving but yet financially unable to secure an education." He envisioned a self-sustaining school where students completed chores in exchange for room and board. Church leaders had difficulty believing that conditions were as dire as described but were finally convinced. Forsythe's dream was realized in 1906 when School of the Ozarks was chartered. The first classes were held in Forsyth, Missouri, the following year.

CORNERSTONE. On October 17, 1906, nearby residents were invited to school grounds to witness the cornerstone of the first building being laid. James Forsythe was a special guest. The stone was provided by the Forsyth Lodge of the Masons, and carvings on its face recognized their contributions. A second stone was laid to recognize contributions from churches. Today, the Masonic stone is housed in the school's museum.

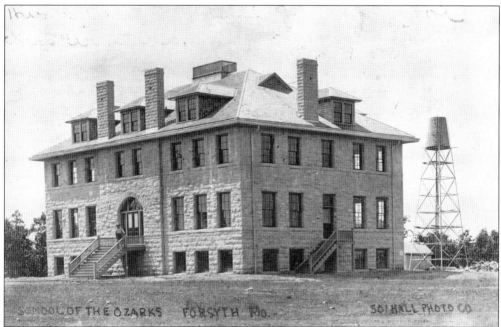

MITCHELL HALL. The first building constructed was Mitchell Hall, named for Kerr Murray Mitchell, a benefactor of the school. It was a multipurpose building. Its four stories and basement served as living quarters, classroom, laundry, dining hall, library, and storage space. There was one toilet in the building, designated for adult staff. Students had to use outdoor facilities.

Clint McDade. McDade was the first student to enroll in 1907, receiving an eighth-grade diploma in 1911. McDade's hobby of growing orchids became a business with greenhouses in the United States and Great Britain. His orchids were a part of Queen Elizabeth's bridal bouquet in 1947. McDade, recipient of the first achievement award from the alumni association in 1950, gave his collection of 5,000 orchids to the college.

Arthur Y. Beatie. Beatie, of Springfield, Missouri, was appointed evangelist to Taney County and responsible for the school project. He raised funds, acquired property, and drew up plans for a campus. As the first principal of S of O, Beatie established the curriculum, which included three departments: literary, industrial, and religious. However, when offered the presidency of the school, Beatie declined and left prior to the school's opening.

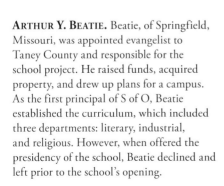

WILLIAM UTTERBACK. Utterback, principal of the school in 1907–1908, is pictured at his desk with Anna Marsh at the desk behind him. Utterback presided over the first students at S of O. He was educated at Wabash College in Indiana and taught high school in Indiana before coming to S of O. Based on the photograph, the office was equipped with a telephone, typewriter, and dictionary.

ANNA MARSH. Anna L. Marsh was the first matron at the School of the Ozarks. She was hired on an interim basis, as Emma Dysart had initially been hired, but she asked to defer her employment for a year while she traveled in Europe. Marsh supervised all household chores and was housemother to all students. She served in that capacity until 1909.

MULE TEAM, 1907. Leonard and Rufus Cummings, pictured here, were the sons of Vincent Cummings of Walnut Shade, Missouri. Vincent was a teacher and farmer who wanted to help the fledgling school develop. He donated the use of his mule team and a wagon for the school's farm work. After driving the mules to S of O and presenting them to Principal Utterback, Cummings walked home.

SCHOOL OF THE OZARKS, 1907. Pictured here are the students, staff, and faculty in 1907. This is the oldest known photograph of the student body. The group is posing outside of Mitchell Hall. Initially, only 16 of the students were boarders. The boys shared two large rooms while the girls did the same. Each student had a bed, a drawer in a shared dresser, and shelf space on the wall.

THE GIRLS OF THE BOARDING DEPARTMENT. The number of boarding students increased from the initial 16 during the school's first year. Pictured here are all the female boarding students in 1907–1908. Anna Marsh, the first matron or housemother, is standing in the center. The girls are posed in front of Mitchell Hall.

THE BOYS OF THE BOARDING DEPARTMENT. Principal W.I. Utterback, on the left, is standing with "his boys." These were the male students who boarded at the School of the Ozarks in 1907–1908. Assistant principal J.A. Oliver is on the right. The coatless boy (third from left) is Johnnie Burns. The other students are unidentified.

INDEPENDENCE HALL. Westminster Presbyterian Church in Independence, Missouri, provided funds for the construction of Independence Hall. It opened in March 1910 and provided faculty housing and office space. The first to move in was Dr. F.O. Hellier, president of the school. On October 21, 1910, a fire in the fireplace spread to the structure. However, the fire was soon extinguished with little damage done.

BOATING AT FORSYTH. The school was located near the White River and Swan Creek, which offered students a break from classes and work. Picnics, swimming, fishing, and boating were all enjoyed by students and faculty. These young ladies are cooling off on a hot July day in 1910. Swan Creek also provided water to the school.

F.O. Hellier, President, 1909–1910. Hellier encouraged students to participate in sports, music, debate, and church organizations. He also felt it important to tell the school's story and established *Our Visitor*, a publication mailed to supporters. It is still published today under the name the *Ozark Visitor*. On Thanksgiving morning of 1909, Hellier's two-year-old son died of illness. Hellier resigned just a few months later.

Hard at Work, c. 1911. Digging a ditch are, from left to right, George Dyer, Arnel Pierce, unidentified, A.J. Buck, and Arlie Blansit. Joseph Gideon is in the wagon holding the reins of the mule team. When he arrived at the school as a new high school enrollee, Buck was given the role of farm superintendent. Buck also won first place in a public speaking contest and played tuba in the band.

PRINT SHOP, 1911. This farmhouse had served as a home, chicken house, corncrib, and toolshed. In 1911, the school was given a printing press, and the building was converted to a printery. Pictured in the doorway is J. Ray King, a student who learned how to run the printing press. King was given a scholarship in exchange for his work as head printer.

S OF O NORMAL STUDENTS, 1911. S of O briefly taught students in a "normal" school or teacher training program, but it was phased out in 1913. Principal George Knepper criticized the effort of the students because nearly half of them failed the teacher's examination. Dr. Knepper is second from the left in the second row. J.A. Oliver is on the far right of the first row.

BASKETBALL. Students at S of O were encouraged to participate in physical activity, especially team sports. Mitchell Hall featured a dirt court with two baskets. Uniforms at the Forsyth campus were a little different than those worn today at Point Lookout, but the school has a long history of successful women's basketball.

BASEBALL TEAM. Posed outside Mitchell Hall are members of the S of O baseball team. Games were played against area town teams. In the third row at center is J.A. Oliver, who was a teacher and principal. It is likely that he was a player/manager for the baseball team given the need for nine players. He is also wearing a catcher's mitt so that may have been his playing position.

BAND, 1913. S of O promoted the arts in its curriculum with public speaking, theatrical productions, and music. The band included brass, woodwinds, and percussion instruments. The man on the left without a hat is Principal J.A. Oliver. He was originally hired in 1908 as assistant principal but was promoted when his predecessor left after just one semester.

PICNICKING ON SWAN CREEK. This photograph, taken on June 8, 1908, includes Mabel Hicks, Edna Vanzandt, Jessie Coulter, Fay Stires, Alice Franklin, Florence Ray, Willie Coulter, Bessie Williams, Marion Wassou, Cornelia Craig, and Eva Eakin. The school's campus was located just up the hill from Swan Creek. On a hot day, the cool breeze off the water and the shade trees were surely a relief.

Joseph Gideon. Gideon was born in a log cabin in Christian County, Missouri, in 1884. He became the first student to receive a high school diploma from the School of the Ozarks when he graduated in 1913. He also received an eighth-grade diploma from S of O in 1909. Although he was the only member of his class in 1913, Gideon received a full commencement ceremony, including the gift of a 21-volume pocket edition of Shakespeare's works. Gideon stayed at S of O as an assistant teacher for one year and then taught at a county school. He eventually attended Cumberland College of Law in Tennessee and had a lengthy career in Taney County as county clerk, prosecuting attorney, and judge. He also boasted that his class of 1913 was the only class where 100 percent of the alumni donated to the school. Gideon's great-grandson Ben Roberts graduated from the College of the Ozarks in 2004. (Courtesy of the Roberts family.)

OUT FOR A WALK. Teachers Mary A. Grace (left) and Cornelia B. Craig (right) are enjoying a stroll with walking sticks in hand. Grace was the school's first librarian and taught Bible classes. Craig taught primary and intermediate students as well as Bible classes. Craig was also a photographer and documented school activities.

HOG BUTCHERING. The School of the Ozarks raised much of its own food, and students participated as part of their work program. In 1910, Bea Farrer (left) and "Pop" Harrison Powell (right) helped butcher hogs. Farrer also played on the school's baseball team. Powell appears to be reading a newspaper in this shot.

POWERSITE DAM UNDER CONSTRUCTION. When S of O opened in 1907, the campus was situated on a hill above the free-flowing White River. In 1910, the Ozark Power and Water Company received congressional authorization to dam the river and chose a site a few miles from the school. Pictured here are members of the construction crew. Completed in May 1913, it was the first hydroelectric dam built in Missouri.

POWERSITE DAM. With the completion of the dam in 1913, Lake Taneycomo was created. Operators of the dam predicted that it would take weeks or even months for the new lake to fill, but it filled in just 30 hours. Lake Taneycomo quickly became a tourist destination. Camp Ozark, where construction workers had lived, was abandoned, and many of the buildings moved to other locations in the area.

A Special Day. Dressed in their finest are S of O students Ethel Stevens (left), Bess Hensley (center), and Neva Coulter (right). September 15, 1909, must have been a special day. Each girl is wearing an S of O armband, and each has a ribbon pinned to her dress. They may have participated in an elocution contest, as prizes were often awarded for those events.

Rev. John Crockett. Crockett was acting president in 1914. An evangelist in Forsyth, he resigned when the school moved to Point Lookout. However, Crockett visited campus frequently and preached when needed on Sundays. He was known as the "Bishop of the Ozarks," with many young men following him into the ministry. Crockett collected Ozarks artifacts and began the campus museum.

Two

The Move to Point Lookout

The cry of "fire" rang out in Mitchell Hall on January 12, 1915. A blaze in the girls' dormitory room spread quickly and consumed the building along with furnishings and personal possessions. No one was seriously injured, but the loss of the building was heartbreaking for School of the Ozarks. Classes were able to resume just a few days later as the Forsyth school offered classroom space. However, with no living quarters, residential students had to make other arrangements. School officials began looking for alternatives.

The loss of Mitchell Hall led to an opportunity. The school's insurance settlement of $15,000 was not enough to rebuild, but a building and property near Hollister were for sale for that same amount. The log building belonged to a hunting and fishing club that had gone bankrupt a few years after moving the structure to Point Lookout. In addition to the building, the property had an orchard, farmland, and a beautiful location overlooking Lake Taneycomo. School officials bought the property.

The log structure, which had served as the exhibit hall for the State of Maine during the 1904 world's fair in St. Louis, was another multipurpose building. Living quarters for students and staff shared space with classrooms, kitchen, and dining room. It was renamed Dobyns Hall in honor of Dr. William Dobyns, a member of the board of trustees.

During the next decade, several buildings were added to the campus. The elementary grades were phased out with the move, but the high school enrollment increased. The frequent turnover of administrators at the Forsyth location ended when Robert M. Good was hired as president. He arrived in 1921 and would remain president until 1952.

Not lost in the fire or the move to Point Lookout was the continued emphasis on the school's mission "to provide the advantages of a Christian education for the youth of both sexes, especially those found worthy, but who are without sufficient means to procure such training."

MITCHELL HALL FIRE. It was a cold January night when Mitchell Hall caught fire. Although the cause of the fire was never determined, suspicion fell on wood stoves used to heat the building or a candle left unattended. Students and staff were evacuated with no injuries, but the building and its contents were a complete loss.

STATE OF MAINE BUILDING. With a $15,000 insurance settlement, S of O purchased the former Maine Hunting and Fishing Club located at Point Lookout near Hollister, Missouri. The club used the building for several years but had gone bankrupt and was forced into foreclosure. In addition to that structure, the property contained 207 acres of farmland with an orchard and a few outbuildings.

MAINE CLUBHOUSE. The State of Maine building at the 1904 world's fair in St. Louis was purchased by a hunting and fishing club. It was disassembled in St. Louis, put on a train to Taney County, and reassembled. When rebuilt, renovations included dividing the second floor into 15 bedrooms. An annex added a kitchen and more bedrooms. The front porch, entry hall, and fireplace remained as they were designed in Maine.

WILLIAM DOBYNS. Dr. William Ray Dobyns was on the board of trustees for the school from 1907 to 1921. When S of O acquired the Maine Clubhouse, the building was renamed to honor the contributions of Dr. Dobyns to the school. As president of the board of trustees, he presided over the dedication of Dobyns Hall on October 28, 1915.

SENIOR CLASS, 1915–1916. Most of the student body made the journey from the Forsyth campus to Point Lookout. Others enrolled for the first time when classes began at Point Lookout. While they appreciated the new campus, it was not perfect. The dorm rooms were not heated and were overcrowded. However, students and staff persisted. This photograph is of the first senior class at Point Lookout in 1915–1916.

ABERNATHY HALL. In 1916, H.T. Abernathy of Kansas City was hunting in the area when he encountered a girl who told Abernathy about S of O. Abernathy visited the campus and decided to donate funds toward a new building. The new facility was ready for use in the fall of 1918. It included dormitory space for boys.

ROBERT M. GOOD. Robert McGowan Good arrived on campus in the summer of 1921 as the newly appointed president of the school. He had degrees from the University of Mississippi. He left a higher-paying job as superintendent of schools in Lexington, Mississippi, to take on the presidency. He was beloved by students and faculty and served as president until 1952, at which time he became president emeritus.

LYTA DAVIS GOOD. Lyta Davis joined the faculty in 1912 while the school was still in Forsyth. She graduated from the University of Arkansas, taught math and biology at S of O, and served as school secretary. She moved with the school to Point Lookout following the fire at Forsyth. On June 25, 1923, Robert M. Good and Lyta Davis married. Their relationship was a surprise to most on campus.

CAMPUS, C. 1919. When the school moved to Point Lookout in 1915, the property included Dobyns Hall as well as sheds and outbuildings. The growing school's most urgent need was dormitory space, and in 1918, Abernathy Hall (left of Dobyns Hall in this photograph) opened with room for 30–40 boys. The path led

from Dobyns Hall to the scenic view of Point Lookout. By the time this photograph was taken, the old Maine sign had been removed from Dobyns Hall and replaced with the letters "S of O." The new sign was a gift from the graduating class of 1916.

Dobyns Hall S of O Hollister M.

DOBYNS HALL. Much like Mitchell Hall in Forsyth, Dobyns Hall was a multipurpose building with dormitories, a dining hall, classrooms, and offices all housed under its roof. When Dr. Good arrived on campus in 1921, he moved into a room screened off on the porch. It was heated with a wood stove, and he had to chop his own wood.

CATHERINE GOOD. The marriage of the Goods produced Catherine Virginia, born May 23, 1924. She is pictured here near Abernathy Hall. Other photographs of Catherine show her in her mother's arms and receiving an Easter bunny. Sadly, she died in 1926, just short of her second birthday. The whole campus mourned Catherine's loss. Catherine was buried in Holly Springs, Mississippi, her father's hometown.

DOBYNS HALL, REAR VIEW. Dobyns Hall faced west toward Point Lookout and Lake Taneycomo. The rear view seen here faced east. A windmill on this side helped provide water while an annex housed a kitchen and storage. The upper floor of the annex served as the boys' dormitory while girls lived on the second floor of the main building.

RELAXING AT DOBYNS HALL. Between classes, homework, and chores, life was busy for S of O students. It was equally busy for faculty and staff who supervised the students, worked a variety of jobs, and worried about how to keep the school going when funds were low. However, there were occasions when everyone could rest. This group is enjoying a quiet Sunday on the porch at Dobyns Hall.

Fire Drill. The Mitchell Hall fire in Forsyth had made S of O officials keenly aware of the need for fire protection. They also recognized that Dobyns Hall, a building constructed with oiled logs and an asphalt roof, was susceptible to fire. This group appears to be drilling with a fire hose, a fire hydrant, and early fire extinguishers.

Stevenson Hall under Construction. When construction on Abernathy Hall was finished, H.T. Abernathy decided to help with another building that would be similar. He donated $10,000, which matched his donation for the previous building. Like Abernathy Hall, Stevenson Hall featured extensive exterior rockwork. That may have required an experienced crew, as the men in this photograph do not appear to be students.

STEVENSON HALL. When completed in 1921, Stevenson Hall contained dormitory space for 60 girls, a kitchen, a dining room, and a laundry. It was named for Mary Stevenson Abernathy in honor of H.T. Abernathy's deceased wife. The building eventually became living quarters for women teachers, although the campus laundry continued to be housed in the basement.

RINGING THE BELL. A typical school day begins with the ringing of a bell, and life at S of O was no different. This bell had been salvaged from the ashes of Mitchell Hall in Forsyth and moved to Point Lookout. It rang to summon students to classes and meals. It is still located on campus.

HOSPITAL. Finished in 1927, Lillian McDonald Hospital was located next to Dobyns Hall. It was named in honor of the daughter of W.A.P. McDonald, who donated funds for the building. The cottage later became the home economics building and was renamed the Anna Lee Perry Building. A rock veneer was added in 1954. In 1980, it was converted into a day care and used until torn down in 1990.

ENTRANCE GATES. S of O's intentional focus on students without the economic means to attend school meant that many students entered S of O with little more than a suitcase and a few clothes. When that student walked through the entrance gates, it was with the knowledge that hard work would be expected but the effort would result in an education that could be life-changing.

GREEN BUILDING. As enrollment grew, facilities at Point Lookout were stretched thin. Consequently, the Allen P. Green Building was constructed and dedicated on April 20, 1928. It housed classrooms, offices, an auditorium, and a gymnasium. There was also a chapel. Until that time, students were often transported to Hollister for church services, or a preacher would address the student body in the crowded Dobyns Hall.

GREEN BUILDING LIBRARY. The school has had a library since its opening. The original collection of donated books was destroyed by the Mitchell Hall fire in 1915. After the Green Building opened in 1929, the library moved from Dobyns Hall to Green. This was a fortuitous move as Dobyns Hall burned down in 1930, and the library would have been lost again had it not been moved.

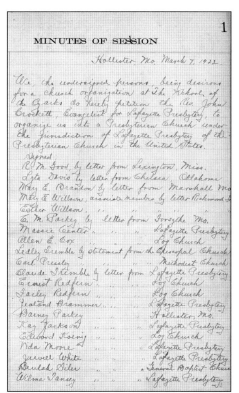

MINUTES OF SESSION

[handwritten petition text]

Hollister Mo. March 7, 1922.

We the undersigned persons, being desirous for a church organization at The School of the Ozarks do hereby petition the Rev. John Crockett, Evangelist for Lafayette Presbytery, to organize us into a Presbyterian church under the jurisdiction of Lafayette Presbytery of the Presbyterian Church in the United States.

Signed
R. M. Good, by letter from Lexington, Miss.
Lyta Davis by letter from Chelsea, Oklahoma
Mary E. Brandon by letter from Marshall Mo
Mary E. Willson, associate member by letter Richmond, Ia.
Esther Willson
E. M. Parkey by letter from Forsythe Mo.
Massie Center   Lafayette Presbytery
Allen E. Cox   Log Church
Ledley Tremble by statement from the Episcopal Church
Earl Presley   Methodist Church
Claude Tremble by letter from Lafayette Presbytery
Ernest Redfern   Log Church
Farley Redfern   Log Church
Jealand Drammer   Lafayette Presbytery
Dainey Parkey   Hollister, Mo.
Kay Jackson   Lafayette Presbytery
Edward Koenig   Log Church
Nda Moore   Lafayette Presbytery
Juewel White   Lafayette Presbytery
Beulah Diler   General Baptist Church
Wilma Vansey   Lafayette Presbytery

CHURCH PETITION. On March 7, 1922, members of the S of O community petitioned the Lafayette Presbytery to establish a Presbyterian church at Point Lookout. The letter was signed by those who planned to transfer their memberships to the new church. Dr. Good and Lyta Davis were the first signees. The petition was granted, and the church organized.

ENTRANCE. Visitors on campus were encouraged but as noted on the sign at the entrance gate, cars were prohibited until 4:00 p.m. on Sundays to avoid disrupting church services. The stone posts and archway are still in their original location, but the road now runs past rather than through the gate, and a sign for Lake Honor hangs beneath the arch.

Boys' Basketball Team. Seated on the porch steps of Dobyns Hall are members of the basketball team along with their bobcat mascot. The bobcat was adopted as the mascot in 1924. Coach Stanley L. Wilson suggested the name after pointing out a taxidermy mount of a bobcat on the fireplace mantel. The nickname stuck, and today's athletic teams are still known as the Bobcats.

Carl Cave. Cave began teaching at S of O in 1927. He taught math, coached athletic teams, supervised the dormitory in Abernathy Hall, coordinated student work, and was the principal and superintendent of the high school. One of his goals was to have a more regular classroom schedule. Until Cave arrived, it was common practice for classes to be dismissed if chores needed to be done.

DOBYNS FIRE. On February 1, 1930, S of O suffered another catastrophe when Dobyns Hall burned. The oil-treated logs and asphalt roof burned hot and quickly with very little able to be salvaged. The entire building was gone in less than an hour. The cause of the fire was undetermined, but suspicion fell on a hot stove. Bertha Collins, a 17-year-old student, was taking a bath when she heard screaming. She got out of the tub, threw on a coat, and headed down the stairs even though the railings were on fire. She made it out unscathed, as did everyone else. Neighbors in Hollister, Branson, and Springfield responded to news of the fire by sending clothing and cash to the school. The loss of the building was estimated at $50,000, but it was insured for just $10,000, which did not include any personal belongings of students and faculty.

Three

THE GREAT DEPRESSION AND WORLD WAR II

While operating the School of the Ozarks had been a challenge since its founding, the loss of Dobyns Hall in 1930 ushered in an especially challenging time. The Great Depression and World War II impacted the school more significantly than previous world events. At that time, S of O needed $150 per day in contributions to operate but with the Depression, many donors found themselves unable to give. The school had accounts at a Hollister bank for payroll and operating expenses, but that bank failed in 1931. Paychecks were sometimes late, and appeals went out for necessities like bedding, work clothes, and a new truck.

Federal programs provided some help. The school had been canning fruits and vegetables for years with a canning factory that could produce 5,000 cans per day. Consequently, the school signed up for a program sponsored by the Federal Relief Commission. S of O's factory canned beef in exchange for funds that were divided between the school and the students who worked in the cannery. The money helped keep the school afloat.

World War II was keenly felt on campus as past and present students enlisted in the armed forces. Newsletters from the school during this time included updates from those serving as well as notes on how the absence of many of the older boys was impacting the school's work program. By 1943, S of O had 250 men and women in the service. Sadly, not all of them made it home.

While the Great Depression and World War II presented challenges, there was good news during those years. Major construction projects were completed with gifts from generous donors. One of the school's most supportive donors, L.W. Hyer, had a tremendous impact on the campus during this era. Many of his contributions can still be seen today.

THOMPSON DINING HALL. The new dining facility opened in 1930 and is the oldest extant building on campus. While visiting for graduation in 1929, Frank and Mattie Thompson witnessed the crowded conditions in Dobyns Hall. They immediately decided to build a new facility. Thompson has also served as a rehearsal hall for the music department and today houses the Christian ministries and counseling departments.

WATER TOWER. Pictured behind the Thompson Dining Hall and Lillian McDonald Hospital is the water tower. Water was pumped up from Lake Taneycomo to the tower. It was a wooden tank on steel legs that was 125 feet tall. It was painted by a student, working solo with no safety equipment. To make the job more challenging, the student had only one arm.

L.W. HYER. An executive with the J.C. Penney corporation, Hyer began serving on the board of trustees in 1928. His support of the school included donating funds for the canning factory, power plant, a herd of Jersey cattle, Lake Honor, the chapel bell tower, and an endowed scholarship fund for students. The school was also the chief beneficiary of Hyer's $15 million estate.

JOHNSON POWER PLANT. The need for central heating had been discussed since the school relocated to Point Lookout, and construction on a power plant got underway in 1929. It was named for Jackson Johnson, chairman of the International Shoe Company. His bequest to the school along with donations from Johnson's friends provided most of the funding. It originally burned coal but today is powered by natural gas.

GREEN BUILDING. When the Green Building was constructed, the college's main entrance was located near where Lake Honor is today. Those entering the campus came through the gate and drove the road pictured here. Today, the road follows the same route but now has the Jones Building and Memorial Hall on either side.

CAMPUS, C. 1931. In just a little more than a decade, the Point Lookout campus underwent many changes. Pictured are, from left to right, the Green Building, Acom Building, Stephenson Hall, Thompson Dining Hall, Lillian McDonald Hospital, Abernathy Hall (behind the hospital), and the Johnson Power Plant. Planted in front is a field of cabbage.

LAKE HONOR. In 1931, a spring-fed stream was dammed to create a small lake. Improvements over the years included a barbecue grill, fountain, fence, a small island with a swan house, and stocking the lake with fish. Water pumped from Lake Taneycomo for use in the power plant was piped to Lake Honor, aerated, and returned to Taneycomo. Lake Honor provided a good place for picnics and swimming.

SNIPPING BEANS. One of L.W. Hyer's gifts was a canning factory in 1928. Modern equipment was leased from the American Canning Company of New York for $1 per year, and by 1931, students were canning up to 5,000 cans of fruits and vegetables a day. When green beans got ripe, everyone pitched in to harvest, snip, and can the beans.

TOMATOES. A youngster is contemplating the work ahead as he looks at bushels of tomatoes. Tomatoes were a cash crop in the Ozarks, with over 200 canneries operating from 1925 to 1945. S of O grew its own tomatoes but also purchased produce from area farmers. The school would furnish seed and fertilizer, with farmers expected to bring their harvest to the school's cannery. (Courtesy of Jody Braswell.)

BASKETBALL TEAM, 1932. By 1932, the women's basketball team had modernized their uniforms while they enjoyed playing against fellow students or other area schools. This team finished its season with thirteen wins and five losses. Victories included winning the S of O tournament by defeating Forsyth. Their motto for the season was "Cooperation Wins."

JAMISON BLDG. SCHOOL OF THE OZARKS PT. LOOKOUT, MO. B-34

JAMISON BUILDING. A gift from board member H.S. Jamison provided funds for the Jamison Manual Training Building. Over the years, the building housed the manual arts facilities, mass communications department, and weaving and stained-glass studios as well as the electronics and security departments. Today, a renovation and addition have transformed the Jamison building into the Watson Student Center.

MAUDE FINCH. Called "Mother Finch," Maude Finch was a widow from St. Joseph, Missouri, who joined S of O in 1914 as matron. When the school moved to Point Lookout, she supervised the girls' dormitory, study halls, and prayer meetings. Finch also ran the charity room where students could exchange work hours for donated clothes. Mother Finch spent more than 40 years working for S of O.

SPARKLING STANDARD SIR. An award-winning bull, Sparkling Standard Sir, was a mainstay of the school's Jersey herd. He was purchased for $25,000 by L.W. Hyer and given to S of O. In addition to winning his own awards, the bull fathered many prize-winning daughters known for their milk production. He is pictured here with dairy manager John Fawcett.

CANNING FACTORY. Canning food was a way to feed students, but it became a campus industry. In 1928, L.W. Hyer bought canning equipment and then in 1938 provided funds for a new building, pictured here. It could produce 20,000 cans per day. Tomatoes, green beans, and other products were sold under the school's label. The canning factory closed in 1968, and the building was converted into the college press.

GEOMETRY CLASS. Students at S of O studied the three Rs. After the primary grades were phased out, high school math included geometry. Carl Cave (left) taught math in addition to fulfilling his responsibilities as principal. For many students, S of O provided educational opportunities that were life-altering and helped lift them out of poverty.

WORKING IN THE FIELDS. Male students at S of O were often assigned to agricultural work. Those pictured here are cutting sorghum to feed the dairy herd. Other livestock included beef cattle, hogs, and poultry. In addition to a truck garden to feed students, faculty, and staff, the school raised crops to feed livestock.

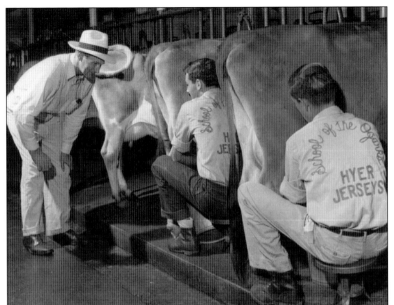

MILKING TIME. Dairy manager John Fawcett supervises the milking of the Hyer Dairy Jerseys. L.W. Hyer was especially fond of the Jersey breed, and the school received much publicity for the herd. The cows were featured in issues of the *Jersey Bulletin*, breeders' conferences were held at the school, and Hyer was honored by the Missouri Jersey Breeders Association.

FRUITCAKE. Annabelle McMaster was hired to oversee the government canning project and teach home economics. At Christmastime, her students were baking fruitcakes. Dr. Good, attracted by the aroma, asked if he could mail cakes to donors. He promised that if any donations were received as a result, he would buy an electric stove for the class to use. Donations came, the stove was bought, and an industry was born.

A FULL STRINGER OF FISH. L.W. Hyer (right) was a lifelong bachelor who became so interested in S of O that he eventually built a house on the campus. Hyer's job with J.C. Penney was based in St. Louis, but he made frequent trips to Point Lookout to keep an eye on his Jersey cows and construction projects. He also went on an occasional fishing trip with Dr. Good (left).

DOC GOOD'S OFFICE. Dr. Good spent hours each day in his office but enjoyed spending time out around campus too. His office featured pictures of his "boys and girls" along with friends of the college. Answering mail took a great deal of time. Every donation to the college, regardless of its size, got a personal response and receipt. He sometimes dictated over 100 letters a day.

SENIOR SQUAD, 1938–1939. From left to right are (first row) Elkanah Wilbanks, Fred Ward, Wellman Caudill, and Claude Moyer; (second row) Elysha Wyatt, Billy Ash, Glen Johnston, and Frank McKinny. The team was known as the "One- or Two-Point Team," as they lost so many close games. However, they did win two good sportsmanship trophies. Wilbanks was killed in the Pacific theater during World War II.

FOSTER DORMITORY. Officially known as Foster-McCarthy Hall, Foster was opened in 1940. It was named in honor of Ione Foster McCarthy, who donated funds for its construction. When opened, two rooms were set aside for guests but that proved inadequate. Realizing that, Foster donated additional funds for a guesthouse, which today is home to the alumni office.

CAMPUS CIRCLE. In the foreground is the bell brought from the Forsyth campus. Stevenson Hall is to the left, and Foster Dormitory is in the center. There are several buildings in the background on the right, but it is unclear what they are. The circle is still a part of the campus landscape, although it looks a little different today.

GOOD FRIENDS. Living and working in close quarters meant that close friendships developed amongst the faculty and staff, and many enjoyed the family atmosphere on the relatively isolated campus. This group includes, from left to right, librarian Allison Prescott, dietitian Ida Williams, and teachers Dorothy Ross, Isabelle Wood, and Mildred LaSieur. The photograph was taken on June 2, 1941.

MEMORIAL DORMITORY. When opened in 1942, this girls' dormitory was known as Memorial because the donor wished to remain anonymous. After her death in 1969, Louisa Maytag Smith was revealed as the benefactor, and her name was added to the building. However, to avoid confusion with the Harriet T. Smith Dormitory constructed in 1957, it continued to be known as Memorial Dorm.

EUGENE "PEACHES" WESTOVER. Peaches spent five years at S of O before receiving a degree from Drury College. He enrolled as an eighth grader after being orphaned in the influenza epidemic of 1918. Both S of O and Drury considered him one of their best basketball players, and he is in the Athletic Hall of Fame at both schools. He was killed during the Battle of the Bulge on December 12, 1944.

Four

EXPANSION OF
THE CAMPUS AND
INTO A COLLEGE

With the end of World War II, life at the School of the Ozarks returned to normal. Students went to classes, work, and chapel while faculty and staff continued the hard work of teaching, supervising, and finding resources to keep the campus going. But in many ways, there was no going back to that prewar existence. Outside influences again impacted the school. When S of O was established in 1906, there were no high schools in the county but that changed during the decades leading up to the war. Public high schools opened in area towns, and better transportation meant those schools were accessible to more students. Consequently, S of O began thinking about its future and the need for higher education in the Ozarks. The school added a junior college in 1956 and expanded to a four-year college in 1966. In 1967, the last high school class graduated as did the first four-year college students. From 1968 until 2012, S of O operated solely as a four-year college. A lab school featuring a classical, Christian curriculum was reinstated in 2012, initially as a high school and now encompassing grades K-12.

Growth of campus facilities continued along with sports, clubs and organizations, and the arts. While some longtime faculty and staff left or retired, new employees were hired, many of whom would spend their careers at the school. One of the most significant of the new hires was Dr. M. Graham Clark. He was initially hired as vice president but assumed the presidency when Dr. Good retired in 1952. Clark served as president for 29 years, overseeing the transition from high school to college. One of Clark's most enduring projects was the construction of Williams Memorial Chapel, completed in 1958. The chapel was built where Dobyns Hall had been located, at the heart of the campus. For the first time in its history, the School of the Ozarks had a dedicated place for students, faculty, and staff to worship.

DR. M. GRAHAM CLARK.
Clark was living in Atlanta, Georgia, when he caught the eye of Dr. Ed Grant, chair of the Committee on Religious Education for the Presbyterian Church. Grant recommended Clark for the vice presidency at S of O. Clark was vice president from 1946 to 1952, at which point he became president. He served in that position until retiring in 1980 and being named president emeritus.

THE SCHOOL OF THE OZARKS									

DETACH BEFORE DEPOSITING

N⁰ 52609 M. Graham Clark

THE SCHOOL OF THE OZARKS
POINT LOOKOUT, (NEAR HOLLISTER) MISSOURI

SECURITY BANK OF BRANSON
BRANSON, MISSOURI

DATE	DESCRIPTION	AMOUNT	DISCOUNT %	AMOUNT	OTHER DEDUCTIONS FOR	AMOUNT	NET AMOUNT
9/28/53	Sept. Salary	$500.00			W. H. S. S.	35.30 4.50	$460.20

CLARK PAY STUB. When he accepted the vice presidency of S of O in 1946, Dr. M. Graham Clark took a pay cut from his job in insurance. His starting salary was $250 per month. At the fall 1952 board of trustees meeting, board members approved a motion to name Dr. Clark president and Dr. Good president emeritus. The salary for both men was set at $500 per month.

J.M. McDonald Machine Shop. Constructed in 1947, the machine shop was one of several buildings funded by the McDonald family. It initially housed equipment for fabricating metal along with other construction needs, but in 1964, it was repurposed as the McDonald Administration Building. The building's location near the main entrance made it an ideal spot to house administrative staff. Construction workers were relocated to other areas of campus.

Josephine Armstrong McDonald Hospital. Opened in 1951, the Josephine McDonald Hospital had 40 beds along with examination rooms on the main floor. The top floor has been used as an additional dormitory. The basement initially housed clothing rooms but was then converted to the library and today is primarily storage space. When the nursing major was established in 2006, the hospital was renovated to provide simulation labs.

BEULAH WINFREY. Winfrey, pictured with her husband, Wayne, joined the faculty in 1948 as a business teacher. When junior college classes were added, Winfrey went back to school to get a master's degree so she could teach at the collegiate level. The school awarded her an honorary doctorate in 1994. She was in her 53rd year of teaching at the school when she died in October 2000.

TYPING CLASS. High school students took typing in addition to more traditional academic subjects. Teacher Beulah Winfrey is standing in the back of the room, which was located in the Green Building. Several brands and models of typewriters are being used. It is likely that most of them were acquired as surplus property.

LIBRARY IN MCDONALD HOSPITAL.
When McDonald Hospital was
constructed, the school's library moved
from the Green Building to the basement
of the hospital. The location was
challenging due to plumbing leaks and
coal dust from the power plant across
the street. However, the move proved
fortuitous when the previous location,
the Green Building, burned down
in 1964.

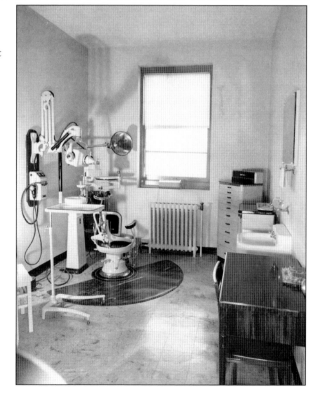

DENTAL HEALTH ROOM. Many
S of O students did not have access to
health care until they arrived at school.
In addition to providing a hospital to
treat minor illnesses and injuries, the
school employed a dentist and brought
in outside health care providers for the
annual tonsillectomy day.

59

BAILEY SCIENCE BUILDING. The Bailey Science Building was funded by Mary Bailey in memory of her husband, Henry. It housed the biology, chemistry, math, and physics departments when opened in 1954. The exterior stone was salvaged from the courthouse and other buildings in Forsyth, Missouri, when Forsyth was moved in 1950 due to the creation of Bull Shoals Lake. Bailey was renovated in 1992 and renamed Berger Hall.

MARIETTA MUSIC TEACHERS COTTAGE. Although gone today, the Marietta Cottage was one of several houses constructed on campus in the 1950s and 1960s. Some were single-family homes; others accommodated multiple tenants. Faculty and staff were encouraged to live on campus, and many of their children have fond memories of growing up on campus. Marietta Cottage was built in 1955.

DR. ALICE A. NIGHTINGALE. Dr. Nightingale was a scientist and teacher who joined S of O in 1955. She previously worked for the Pineapple Research Institute in Honolulu and was an eyewitness to the bombing of Pearl Harbor in 1941. Nightingale developed the science curriculum and laboratories for the junior college. She published a book on daisies of the Ozarks and always wore a flower in her hair.

J.C. PENNEY. Longtime benefactor L.W. Hyer worked for the J.C. Penney corporation and brought the school to Penney's attention. Pictured here attending a Rotary Conference held on campus in 1955, J.C. Penney himself became a benefactor of the school. In addition to funds, Penney sent unsold clothing and shoes from his chain of stores to S of O for distribution to students.

HARRIETT T. SMITH DORMITORY. Known as Smith Dorm, this facility opened in 1957 to house male students. There were also apartments on the ground floor for married faculty. The dormitory was renovated in 1987 and renamed the Youngman Dormitory and Conference Center. The basement housed conference facilities and a writing center. Those would eventually be moved elsewhere, and today, the entire building is dedicated to dormitory space.

MAILING FRUITCAKES. As sales of fruitcakes grew, so did the mailing operations to get them delivered. Pictured here are boxes of fruitcakes being delivered to the post office. From 1931 to 1972, the post office was located on the bluff by Point Lookout. Limited parking and space necessitated a move to the current location near the administration building.

WILLIAMS MEMORIAL CHAPEL. Chapel services were always a part of campus life, but the school never had a dedicated space to worship until Williams Memorial Chapel was constructed. Former US senator George Williams of Florida provided the financing. The initial project foreman was William Johnson, who had also worked on Hollister's English architecture on Downing Street. S of O's Harding Wyman and Clarence Parkey completed the work. Construction was done by students using rock quarried on campus. All the woodwork was designed by James Jamison, head of the campus furniture factory. The neo-Gothic chapel is 150 feet long by 80 feet wide and in the shape of a recumbent cross. A crypt was built into the basement for the interment of school presidents. However, the crypt was never used and was eventually converted into storage space. The building was dedicated on May 1, 1958, complete with stained glass, pipe organ, and bells.

CHAPEL INTERIOR. The interior of the chapel featured pews made in the school's furniture factory. The stained-glass windows were manufactured by the firm of Gianinni and Hilgart in Chicago. Images on the windows feature a chronology of Biblical history. Many students will recall the opening of Sunday chapel services when the lights were switched on in synchronization with the chapel bells.

CHAPEL CONGREGATION. Students were required to attend chapel services, a practice that continues today. Services were also open to members of the local community. Dr. Clark became a licensed Presbyterian minister so that he could officiate at services, weddings, and other events. Although affiliated with the Presbyterian Church, services have always been open to worshippers of all denominations.

S OF O TRUCK. Parked next to the Bailey Building and across from the canning factory is one of the school's trucks. Much of the equipment and vehicles needed for campus operations were donated or purchased from surplus property sales. The school was able to acquire secondhand goods because it had employees who were skilled at making repairs or adaptations.

CUTTING STONE. In the early years, the stone used in campus construction was quarried on campus. Students participated in the entire process. They worked in the limestone quarry, cut rock into blocks, and constructed the buildings. Lyons Memorial Library, opened in 1964, was the last building on campus made of stone quarried on campus.

FURNITURE FACTORY. Having a student workforce meant that products could be manufactured on campus rather than purchased. That included furniture. The first furniture made on campus was used in Smith Dormitory when it opened in 1957. The furniture factory also made tables and chairs for the library. In 1960, a new and improved furniture factory was built.

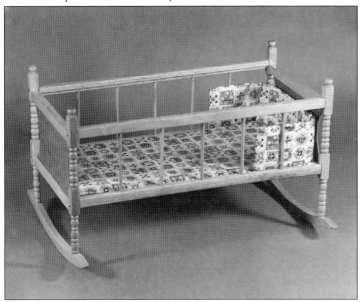

DOLL CRADLE. The cradle pictured here was made in the furniture factory as part of a contract with an outside company. An accompanying piece was a doll bunk bed. Children's furniture, such as rocking chairs, were also produced. One of the doll cradles is preserved in the college's archival collection.

CAMPUS, C. 1960. This view provides glimpses of buildings that have disappeared. Located between the power plant and Thompson Dining Hall are several small buildings, including a greenhouse. Across the street is the original hospital. Stephenson Teachers Cottage, on the far left, was torn down to make way for a new library. The faculty and staff homes left of Smith Dormitory are now gone. Other buildings in the photograph are still in use but have been renovated and, in some cases, renamed. Those include the Jordan Music Building, Hyer Canning Factory, McDonald Print Shop, Bailey Science Building, McDonald Machine Shop, and Jamison Building, all located in the foreground of this photograph. Lake Taneycomo is visible in the top left corner. The empty field at the top of the photograph eventually became home to the athletic complex. Many of the changes to those existing buildings happened in the decade after this image was taken.

SUMMER THEATER. In 1955, students from Southern Illinois University opened a summer theater in Branson. One of the plays in their repertoire was *The Shepherd of the Hills*, based on the novel by Harold Bell Wright, a book often credited as the origin of Branson's tourism industry. School of the Ozarks acquired the theater in 1961. *The Mikado* by Gilbert and Sullivan was on the playbill that summer.

NEW LIBRARY. When college accreditors toured the campus in 1961, they asked when an adequate library would be built. Dr. Clark had a work crew dig out the basement during the night and showed the accreditors the spot the next morning as evidence that construction was imminent. The accrediting team was impressed and noted the progress in their final report.

MOVING BOOKS, DECEMBER 1963. One of the last jobs to be completed before the new library opened was moving the book collection from the basement of the hospital. Campus jobs closed for the day, and everyone helped with the move. Large furniture was moved by truck, but smaller items and all the books were carried by students.

LYONS MEMORIAL LIBRARY. The newly finished library opened in January 1964. It was named for Morris and Hazel Lyons, major benefactors of the project. Furniture was made in the campus furniture factory, with study tables and chairs lining the windows on the perimeter. The basement included the campus bookstore and a faculty lounge while the top floor was empty, awaiting future growth.

FESTIVAL OF ARTS. With the new library open, S of O celebrated its first annual Festival of Arts. This nine-day celebration included art exhibits, concerts, theatrical productions, lectures, and campus tours. Dr. Clark (left) welcomed a special guest, artist Thomas Hart Benton (right). Artwork was hung on the library's vacant top floor during the festival.

WORK AS CLASSROOM. From the beginning of the school, students and supervisors have worked alongside each other. Whether in the machine shop, as pictured here, or in one of the other workstations on campus, students learn many skills from experienced leaders. Some students used that campus job as a springboard to a career.

BARNS. Because of the school's extensive agricultural programs, barns and other outbuildings have been a necessary part of campus. These barns were located on the east side of campus but have since been torn down and replaced. The water tower is visible in the background. It has also been torn down.

MCDONALD ADMINISTRATION BUILDING. The machine shop was renovated to become the administration building due to its central location. Wings were added at each end of the building, with the front of the structure moved to face east toward Lake Honor. The decorative solar shades matched those on the newly built library.

GREEN BUILDING FIRE. Another disastrous fire occurred on December 26, 1964, when the Green Building burned. Ironically, the building was funded by Allen P. Green who became a millionaire by selling fire brick. The school was on Christmas break but students who had remained on campus discovered the fire and sounded the alarm. The campus fire department was aided by departments from Hollister, Branson, and Forsyth but the building was a total loss. Included in the loss was equipment for the US Naval Reserve Unit, which had been organized on campus in 1961. The unit was forced to temporarily disband until equipment could be replaced. Another major loss was student enrollment records and alumni files. Because of the fires at Mitchell Hall, Dobyns Hall, and the Green Building, it can still be hard to verify student enrollment from the first half of the school's history. Within hours of the fire, Dr. Clark asked the campus architect to draw up plans for a replacement building and made contingency plans for classes.

Five

THE COLLEGE
THAT WORKS

With the graduation of the last high school students in 1967, the School of the Ozarks was fully involved in higher education. The four-year program was given preliminary accreditation by the North Central Association in 1965, with full accreditation coming in 1971. Growth continued on the physical campus but also in the programs of study. The faculty doubled in size as new majors were added. In 1973, for the first time in years, the board of trustees voted to amend the college's goals by adding patriotism to the existing academic, vocational, spiritual (since renamed Christian), and cultural goals.

Growth did not come without growing pains though. The years of construction took a financial toll, and in October 1968, the board of trustees passed a resolution that no new construction would begin until sufficient funds were in hand to complete projects. Nationally, it was a time of protests on college campuses. There were a few protests at Point Lookout but most related to what were perceived as "high school" rules governing curfew, cars, beards, and a green line that divided the boys' side of campus from the girls' side.

The growth of tourism in the Tri-Lakes area meant that the campus saw more visitors. Facilities, especially directed towards those visitors, included the Friendship House and Rose O'Neill Tea Room, Beacon Hill Theatre, Ralph Foster Museum, and Edwards Mill. An airport was also constructed, available to both travelers and students enrolling in the new aviation science program.

The college's learn-as-you-work program always garnered attention, but on March 15, 1973, the story went national when the *Wall Street Journal* published an article about the school and coined the nickname "Hard Work U." The moniker stuck, and today, the college often refers to itself as "Hard Work U."

KSOZ-FM. February 10, 1962, was an auspicious day as the school's radio station, KSOZ, first went on the air. The FM station originally broadcast from the chapel basement and produced much original content. The station was a charter member of National Public Radio (NPR) in 1970 but dropped that affiliation in 1989. The call sign was changed to KCOZ when the School of the Ozarks became the College of the Ozarks in 1990.

HOLSTEINS, 1963. The dairy herd changed from Jerseys to Holsteins in 1963 when the W. Alton Jones Holstein Dairy Herd was established with an up-to-date milking parlor and barn. W. Alton and Nettie Marie Jones were longtime benefactors of the school but preferred the Holstein breed. Today's herd has Holsteins, Jerseys, and Guernseys.

AN AUDIENCE FOR MILKING. The new milking parlor provided for the W. Alton Jones herd included windows so that visitors could watch the process. Cows are milked twice a day with milk pasteurized and bottled for use in the cafeteria. It is also used to make ice cream sold at the college's restaurant.

BEACON HILL THEATRE. After acquiring the downtown theater in 1961, S of O moved the summer theater to campus and opened it in 1964 as Beacon Hill Theatre. The name came from an aircraft beacon light that was illuminated on show nights to attract audiences. Improvements over the years included enclosing the building and adding air-conditioning. Beacon Hill fell victim to an unidentified arsonist in 1986.

JONES BUILDING. When the Green Building burned in 1964, plans were immediately drawn up for a replacement that would provide classrooms and a theater. The Jones Building was the result. Nettie Marie Jones provided money for construction. In a nod to history, the curved rock wall in the foyer of the theater was made of stone salvaged from the Green Building.

COLLEGE ENTRANCE, 1965. The current entrance to campus was constructed in 1965 as the third in the school's history. The first was near Lake Honor, and the second was located west of today's Veterans Grove. Today, the entrance reads, "College of the Ozarks," while the original "School of the Ozarks" sign has been moved to a spot near Point Lookout.

HELEN AND TOWNSEND GODSEY. Townsend Godsey came to the college in 1965 as public relations director. He also taught journalism and worked as a freelance author and photographer. Godsey began his journalism career as a newspaper reporter and later became the founding editor of the *Missouri Conservationist* magazine. His most well-known work is a collection of photographs titled *These Were the Last*. It features black-and-white photographs of Ozarks natives and their traditions. His interest in the Ozarks also led him to establish the Ozarkiana archival collection at the college's library. The collection includes Godsey's images, photographs and letters from noted folklorist Vance Randolph, and letters written by artist Rose O'Neill to Randolph. The Godsey's coauthored *The Flight of the Phoenix,* a history of the School of the Ozarks published in 1984. Their daughter Maryia, or "Pidge," ran the school's mail room for many years.

FRIENDSHIP HOUSE. Opened in 1968, the Friendship House welcomed campus visitors. It housed the Rose O'Neill Tea Room, a gift shop, and was the boarding point for the campus tour train. Rose O'Neill, the creator of the Kewpie doll, had a home near Branson, and the tearoom featured Kewpie-decorated place mats. The restaurant closed in 2004. Today, the building houses the public relations department and serves as a welcome center.

TOUR TRAIN. In 1967, Nettie Marie Jones gave the school a train. She acquired the engine and four cars from a ski resort in Lake Placid, New York. When the train arrived in Point Lookout, sled runners were changed to wheels and the train was put into service for campus tours. Stops included Edwards Mill and the Ralph Foster Museum, with students providing commentary. The train was retired in 1987.

RALPH FOSTER MUSEUM. The school established a museum in the 1920s. Ozarks radio pioneer Ralph Foster was an enthusiastic collector who donated many of his artifacts to the museum. The facility was renamed in his honor in the 1960s. Foster (right) is shown here with museum director Steve Miller (left) as they examine a Gatling gun.

SIGN ON THE HIGHWAY. As area highways developed, the school added signs to direct visitors to campus. The styles varied as signs were updated. This sign most likely replaced a neon sign installed in the 1950s. Both welcomed visitors, but this version encouraged a trip to the Ralph Foster Museum while on campus.

LAST HIGH SCHOOL GRADUATES. Pictured here in 1967 are the last high school graduates of the original School of the Ozarks. The graduates are flanked by Pres. M. Graham Clark on the left and high school principal Albert Cummings on the right. Cummings was himself a high school graduate from S of O in 1931. Dr. Clark's daughter Julia is in the second row of students, third from the left.

FIRST COLLEGE GRADUATES. Pictured on the steps of the chapel are the first college graduates in 1967. Many of these students also graduated from the junior college, and some had graduated high school. After the construction of the chapel, graduation ceremonies were held there until the event outgrew the space and was moved to the gymnasium.

LAKE HONOR FOUNTAIN. The fountain in Lake Honor is named in honor of Lyta Davis Good, who died in 1963 after serving at the school since 1912. The fountain is illuminated with red, white, and blue lights. Buildings in the background are, from left to right, Edwards Mill, the Landscaping Building, and the farm manager's residence.

THE MIGHTY WURLITZER. Donated to the school in 1969, the Mighty Wurlitzer pipe organ starred in concerts and theatrical productions. College organist Burt Buhrman became known for his Mighty Wurlitzer concerts. Pictured around the organ are members of the music and theater departments. From left to right are (first row) Jean Parnell, Burt Buhrman, and Jean Fry; (second row) John Mizell, Mary Elizabeth Bradley, Luis Rojas, and James Meikle.

FIELDHOUSE, 1969. After the Green Building burned in 1964, a temporary gymnasium was used until this structure opened in 1969. As shown in this photograph, the track was in front of the gym; it is now behind the gym. The pool, in the foreground with windows, was originally outdoors. It opened in 1961 with the enclosure completed in 1967. Today, the gym has been enlarged and is known as the Howell Keeter Athletic Complex. Some buildings in the background are still part of the campus landscape. In the top right next to the tree line is the Transportation Building, while just in front of it is the Alumni Laundry. Left of the laundry is the warehouse. Left of that is the furniture factory, which at various times also housed a cabinet shop, clockmaker, and stained-glass department. Eventually, the structure was given to the industrial education program and referred to as the Technology Building. Today, it is the core of the engineering facilities.

Gym Marquee. This sign, located on a corner next to the gymnasium, provided information on upcoming sporting events. The bobcat sculpture in front had a hedge planted underneath it to simulate fur. The hedge did not always thrive, and the bobcat has since been replaced with a bronze sculpture located closer to the gym entrance.

Chapel Choir. Every Sunday, the chapel choir performs in Williams Memorial Chapel as part of the worship service. They provide special music and lead congregational singing. Dr. John Mizell (first row, left) led the choir for many years and coauthored the "School of the Ozarks Hymn," performed in chapel and at graduations. Organist Bert Buhrman is on the far right in the first row.

ELMER BRASWELL. Reading blueprints was a common activity for Elmer Braswell. He was hired in 1969 as the director of construction. The gymnasium was the first project on which he worked. The growth of the college meant more buildings, more skilled labor, and more student workers for Braswell to manage. He retired in 1995, leaving a significant impact on the campus.

JODY BRASWELL. When Elmer Braswell was hired in 1969, he moved his family to campus. Son Jody, seen here with his first fish, grew up at Point Lookout. When Elmer retired in 1995, Jody took over as director of construction. All construction projects from 1969 to the present have been under the supervision of the Braswell family. (Courtesy of Jody Braswell.)

AIRPORT. The college built its own airport, in large part due to interest from Dr. Clark and Dr. William Todd, a former military pilot who joined the school's administration in 1959. The airport was dedicated on May 1, 1970. An aviation science major was added, and students could earn a pilot's license. In 1977, the airport was named for Dr. Clark.

PAT NIXON. First Lady Pat Nixon visited the college on March 5, 1970. As her motorcade drove onto campus, 100 students holding American flags greeted her. First Lady Nixon toured the campus, ate dinner in the campus cafeteria with students, and planted a pine tree in front of the library. Here, she signs autographs for a group of Brownies while the media looks on.

GOOD COLLEGE CENTER. Named for Robert M. and Lyta Davis Good, the college center was completed in 1973. Its functions have changed over the years. It has housed a motel, bowling alley, chapel, administrative offices, and the student government. Today, it is home to the cafeteria, snack bar, bookstore, and S of O high school. The island and structure in the lake provide a home for swans, while the monument in the foreground commemorates the Lake Honor Award recipients. The award was established in 1931 by L.W. Hyer to recognize students for good citizenship. The marker pictured here was replaced in 1985 to allow more room for names. The smaller marker in the center of the photograph acknowledges Lyta Good and a donor who helped provide the fountain in the lake, not pictured here. A fence was added around Lake Honor in 1986.

KELCE DORMITORY. Gladys Kelce provided funds for building the Russell C. Kelce Dormitory for Men; it is known today as Kelce East and was dedicated in 1970. A matching wing, called Kelce West, was finished in 1981. Walter Haskew, the school's architect, designed the dormitory. It was one of several buildings he designed for the school during the 1960s.

HOWELL KEETER. Dr. Keeter (seated, left) was hired in 1970 as a work program coordinator and would have other titles during his more than 50 years of service. Keeter was an ardent supporter of the Bobcats and Arkansas Razorbacks and was presented with a Razorbacks toilet seat for his 46th birthday. To his right is President Clark. In the background are secretaries Ruth Raley (left) and Shirley Ross (right).

POST OFFICE. On May 27, 1931, a federal post office opened on campus and the 65726 zip code was established for Point Lookout. Mail had previously been picked up in Hollister. Originally located on the bluff overlooking Lake Taneycomo, the post office moved in 1972 to the former McDonald Printing Department.

EDWARDS MILL. Designed to look like a 19th-century gristmill, Edwards Mill was constructed in 1972. Alice and Hubert Edwards, who worked in the flour business, provided the funding. Several historical components were incorporated into the construction, including the millstones and iron hubs of the waterwheel. A mural inside the mill shows the locations of other area mills.

Tiffany Window. The Good College Center was dedicated in 1974, providing space for a cafeteria, auditorium, bowling alley, bookstore, motel, and chapel. The chapel featured a Tiffany stained-glass window titled "The Sower," a gift from Nettie Marie Jones. Today, the window is in the Collins prayer chapel in the Christian Ministries Building.

Weaving Studio. The school established a weaving program in 1937, and it moved to different spots on campus before finding a home on the top floor of Edwards Mill. Some of the first looms were World War II surplus, provided by the federal government. Weaving products included place mats and shawls, with baskets also available.

DINING HALL. Food is always an important consideration for college students. The Thompson Dining Hall served three meals a day until dining facilities were moved to the Good College Center in 1984. The verse on the wall was hung during Dr. Good's presidency. It still hangs today in the current cafeteria.

FIRE CHIEF LARRY COOPER. The campus fire department was established around 1947 because of the school's history of devastating fires. The department was staffed by students with an upperclassman serving as chief. Chief Larry Cooper is pictured here in 1975, the same year that the McDonald Fire House was built. When the alarm sounded, firefighters raced from work or class to respond with campus fire trucks.

VOLLEYBALL TEAM, 1976. Based on the trophies in the photograph, the volleyball team had a successful year in 1976. Coach Marilyn Graves (third row, far right) established and coached the team. She also coached basketball, tennis, and cross-country while teaching physical education. Graves later became dean of the college. A gymnasium in the athletic complex is named in her honor.

AL WALLER. Coach Al Waller joined the faculty in 1977. He coached, taught physical education and math classes, and served as the athletic director. Waller (right) is seen here supervising a student's workout. Waller worked at C of O for 37 years and spent 25 years as head coach of the men's basketball team. The basketball court is named the Al Waller Family Court.

POINT LOOKOUT. Located on the west side of campus, Point Lookout overlooks Lake Taneycomo and Branson. The name "Point Lookout" was suggested by school nurse Constance Downs around 1931 when the post office was established. The panoramic view was her inspiration. The Branson skyline has changed over the years, but the southwest view from Point Lookout still looks remarkably like this photograph. The view to the northwest has seen much more change as the city of Branson has grown. The pump house that draws water from the lake for campus use is located at the foot of Point Lookout, and generations of students have made the trip up or down the bluff. Today, Point Lookout is a popular stop for campus visitors as well as students, faculty, and staff. Point Lookout has also served as a backdrop for weddings, classes, photography shoots, and contemplation.

Six

NEIGHBORS IN BRANSON AND HOLLISTER

The College of the Ozarks campus is located two miles south of Branson, Missouri, and adjacent to Hollister, Missouri. Consequently, the school has a long history with both communities. Hollister was incorporated in 1910, with Branson in 1912, so both were well established when S of O moved to the Point Lookout campus in 1915. Since Hollister was the closer town, its post office served the campus until Point Lookout got its own post office. Students were taken to Hollister for church services. Members of the faculty and staff joined area civic groups, lending their expertise to a variety of causes.

Branson and Hollister are small towns, but millions of tourists are drawn to the area each year. The tourism industry began to develop in the late 19th century as people sought recreation on the White River; however, the publication of the book *The Shepherd of the Hills* in 1907 brought tourism to the forefront. The story was set in the Ozarks, and the popularity of the book caused readers to want to see the locale. Dams were built on the White River, creating Lake Taneycomo, Bull Shoals Lake, and Table Rock Lake. Although the dams inundated the river, new tourism opportunities were created on the lakes. Silver Dollar City and Shepherd of the Hills theme parks opened in the mid-20th century. Local musicians created music shows and began to develop the Branson Strip west of the historic downtown. Following a story about Branson on the television newsmagazine *60 Minutes* in 1991, the "Branson Boom" brought even more development and tourists to the area. Hollister's growth has been less dramatic, but it is still an important neighbor to the college. Students have worked part-time jobs in the area and enjoy the recreational, shopping, and worship opportunities available nearby. Meanwhile, many of the tourists find their way to C of O for a tour of campus.

BOAT LANDING, BRANSON. Waterways have always been important to Branson, whether it be the White River or Lake Taneycomo. This landing in downtown Branson was home to the *Lady of the Lake* and the *Sadie H.*, among other boats. S of O students had fond memories of excursions on some of these boats.

MARVEL CAVE. Early miners believed that the cave contained marble and named it Marble Cave. No marble was discovered, but in 1894, the cave opened as a tourist attraction. In 1927, the name was changed to Marvel Cave. The cave was leased in 1950 by the Herschend family, and today, it is at the heart of Silver Dollar City.

American Pencil Factory. Branson, Mo.

PENCIL FACTORY. The American Pencil Factory in Branson provided significant industry for the area. Cedar trees were harvested and cut into small slats, which were then shipped elsewhere to be made into pencils. The factory began operations around 1909. Branson was also an important producer of railroad ties made of oak.

BRANSON HOTEL. Built in 1903, the Branson Hotel became a stopping point for important Branson visitors. Missouri governor Herbert Hadley (first row in a vest) often visited Branson and was credited with popularizing float fishing. The Branson Hotel is still in business at its original location west of Lake Taneycomo in downtown Branson.

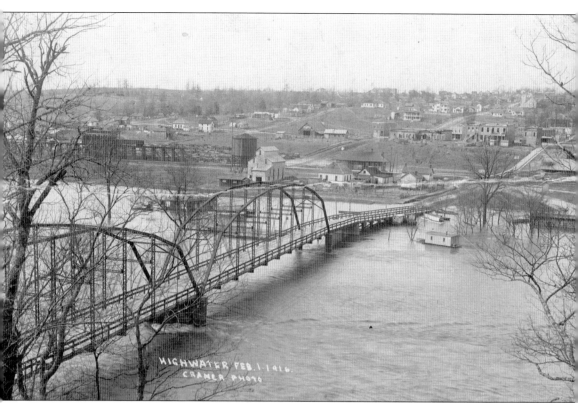

HIGHWATER FEB. 1-1916.
CRAMER PHOTO

BRANSON. S of O's location in Point Lookout was just two miles south of Branson, Missouri, a tourist destination that today hosts millions of visitors each year. This photograph, taken on February 1, 1916, shows flooding in Branson, which was common before Table Rock Dam was built in the 1950s. Branson was incorporated on April 1, 1912, but just months later, a fire on August 29 destroyed almost all the buildings in the downtown business district. Only four buildings survived. They included the Branson Hotel, a bank, a saloon, and the railroad depot. The depot is near the center of this photograph and is still in use today as the boarding location for the Branson Scenic Railway. The bridge in this photograph is long gone, while the Branson Landing retail development occupies the area along the lakeshore.

UNCLE MATT. Harold Bell Wright's book *The Shepherd of the Hills*, published in 1907, was set in the Ozarks. J.K. Ross, the postmaster at Garber, Missouri, served as the inspiration for the character of Uncle Matt. The book's popularity generated a tourism boom as readers wanted to see the locations in the book. An outdoor play adapted from the book has been performed in Branson for decades.

PEARL SPURLOCK. One of the Ozarks's most interesting characters is Pearl Spurlock. She worked for nearly 30 years as a taxi driver and tour guide in the Branson area. Spurlock also published a book called *Over the Old Ozark Trails in the Shepherd of the Hills Country.* This photograph was autographed to her friend and Branson mayor Jim Owen.

SYCAMORE LOG CHURCH. The small log church opened in 1933 near Garber, Missouri, just west of Branson. The town is gone now, but the church is still there and operating. The first pastor was John Crockett, who had been president of the School of the Ozarks from 1914 to 1915. During his time at Sycamore Log Church, Crockett often brought S of O students to worship services.

BRANSON FLOOD. The Hotel Malone and Café are pictured on the left while the sign on the electric pole points toward the ice plant. Train tracks are visible in the foreground. The Malone was one of three early hotels in Branson that catered to visitors. It changed its name to the White River Hotel in 1937.

JIM OWEN. Prominent businessman Jim Owen had a number of business ventures but is most known for his guided float trips and a movie theater in downtown Branson. He also served as mayor of Branson for 12 years. Owen scheduled matinee showings in his theater, especially for S of O students.

GETTING READY FOR A FLOAT. Jim Owen's float business provided fishing guides, boats, and groceries. Clients had to provide their own tackle but were encouraged to buy it at Owen's sporting goods store in Branson. Owen, center in a white shirt, and his guides are shown here outside Ye English Inn in Hollister as they prepare to pick up clients for a trip.

SKAGGS HOSPITAL. Branson did not have a hospital until 1950. M.B. Skaggs, founder of the Safeway chain of stores, challenged the Branson area to raise funds for construction. Skaggs promised to match whatever amount was raised. The hospital was named for Skaggs, but a partnership with CoxHealth in 2013 led to a name change. Today, the hospital is known as Cox Branson.

DEWEY SHORT. Table Rock Dam was proposed years before it was built in 1958. Congressman Dewey Short threw his support behind the project and was instrumental in getting funding for the project. The dam helped with flooding but also created Table Rock Lake, an important part of today's tourism industry. Dewey Short is third from the left in this photograph, pointing out the future location of the dam.

ROTARY CLUB. Dr. Clark was an active member of the Rotary Club at both the local and national levels. Several Rotary conferences were held on the S of O campus. Shown here is the Branson Rotary, dressed for a minstrel show. Dr. Clark, seated in the center and wearing a top hat, served as emcee for the event.

PLUMB NELLIE DAYS. The Plumb Nellie Days festival celebrates art, crafts, food, and music and has been part of the Branson calendar since the mid-20th century. Dr. M. Graham Clark, S of O president, is pictured in the back seat, right. Missouri governor John Dalton is seated directly in front of Clark. The photograph was taken in May 1962. Longtime Branson business Davidson's Jewelry is behind the car.

ANCHOR TRAVEL VILLAGE. Branson's tourism industry has always been an economic driver. The Anchor Travel Village opened in 1936, overlooking Lake Taneycomo. Its clientele was primarily overnight guests who were traveling on Highway 65. The village included a 24-hour restaurant. It began with three cottages, but more were added in later years. Most of the buildings were demolished in the 1970s.

CHULA VISTA. This roadside business on the outskirts of Branson catered to tourists. It featured a gas station, refreshments, cottages, a gift shop that sold baskets, and a free observation tower. The business was on a hill named after Chula Vista, California. Chula Vista in Missouri opened around 1930 and closed in the late 1960s or early 1970s when Highway 65 was realigned to a more easterly route.

ADORATION PARADE. The annual Christmas parade in Branson is called the Adoration Parade. It was the brainchild of businessman Joe Todd and artist Steve Miller (holding picture). Miller later became the museum director at S of O and is well-known for creating the large nativity scene illuminated during the parade. Dr. M. Graham Clark (left of Miller) acts as emcee.

TANEYHILLS LIBRARY. Opened in 1933, the Taneyhills Library began as a project of a women's Sunday school class at the Branson Presbyterian Church. It operated for decades as a volunteer facility, relying on donations, a thrift shop, and proceeds from the book *The Shepherd of the Hills*. The library shared space in the Branson Community Center with the American Legion until moving to its own building in 1977.

TANEY COUNTY TOOTER. The artwork of the Taney County Tooter adorned the wall of a local restaurant. Prices were considerably cheaper when this photograph was taken. The tourism industry meant that motels and restaurants were always an important part of the local economy. Although Branson has its share of chain restaurants today, there are still several locally owned establishments in town.

BALDKNOBBERS. The first regular music show in Branson was performed by the Baldknobbers, who rented the basement of the community center in 1959 for two shows a week. The Presley family performed in a cave near Kimberling City before building a theater on Highway 76 west of downtown Branson in 1967. The Baldknobbers built their own theater in 1968, and the "Strip" was born.

Dairy Trophies. The dairy at the school has been recognized many times for the quality of the herd and milk. Seen here examining trophies from the 1967 Empire District Fair in Springfield, Missouri, are Ben Parnell (left) and S of O president M. Graham Clark (right). Parnell was the founder of People's Bank in Branson and an advocate for the Branson tourism industry.

Christmas Parade. S of O students have been regular participants in the Branson Christmas parade, held every year on the first Sunday evening in December. Some parades have featured floats made by students, the chapel choir singing carols, or, as in this parade, the campus fire truck and firefighters.

SHRINERS. The Branson Shriners frequently take part in the Adoration Parade. This civic organization raises money for the Shriners Children's Hospitals. They are known for driving small cars in parades across the country to attract attention to their cause. These Shriners are driving down Main Street in downtown Branson. A longtime landmark, the Shack Café, is visible in the background.

BEVERLY HILLBILLIES. In 1969, episodes of the television show *The Beverly Hillbillies* were filmed at the Silver Dollar City theme park. Producer Paul Henning had visited Branson as a boy. The cast is pictured here with Branson mayor and businessman Jim Owen. In 1976, Henning gave the show's iconic truck to the Ralph Foster Museum at C of O, where it is a featured exhibit.

DAVIS AND HERSCHEND.
Pres. Jerry Davis (left)
presents Jack Herschend
(right) with a certificate
recognizing contributions
to Free Enterprise Day in
1992. Herschend and his
family own the theme park
Silver Dollar City. There is
a long-standing relationship
between the school and the
park. Herschend's wife,
Sherry, graduated from
S of O in 1950, and the
college is co-owner of a key
piece of property at Silver
Dollar City.

LAKE TANEYCOMO. This photograph provides another view of a flooded Lake Taneycomo. Today, the Branson Landing occupies the lakeshore while four bridges span the lake. Faintly visible at the top of the photograph is Table Rock Dam. Lake Taneycomo winds from that dam to Powersite Dam, looking more like the White River than a lake.

HOLLISTER. This early photograph of Hollister includes the train station in downtown Hollister. What was then Front Street (now Downing Street) in Hollister was originally an alley, but city leaders convinced businesses on the street to reorient buildings so that the front doors faced the train station. Business owners were also asked to use an English architectural style. The hope was to catch the eye of disembarking passengers.

PRESBYTERIAN HILL. An important part of Hollister's geography is the hill overlooking downtown. In 1910, the Presbyterian Assembly of the Southwest bought property on the hill and established a summer retreat. President of the Assembly Rev. George P. Baity is standing behind Pulpit Rock. The relationship with the retreat is likely why the first church in Hollister was Presbyterian.

HOLLISTER PRESBYTERIAN CHURCH. Students from S of O often attended services at this church, located near the Hollister train station. The church was organized in 1911 with construction on the building finished in 1917. Students referred to the church as "one of the most beautiful churches in southwest Missouri." The rock walls were made from rock quarried on-site and complemented the English architecture in downtown Hollister.

LOG CABIN HOTEL. This hotel in Hollister was located just up the hill from the train depot. It featured 20 rooms and a restaurant. Trains would stop in Hollister for a meal break, and passengers would often make the short walk to the hotel to dine. The Log Cabin Hotel was in business for about 30 years before it burned.

MAIN STREET, HOLLISTER. City leaders in Hollister decided early in the town's history to market to visitors traveling by train. In addition to facing businesses toward the depot and redecorating in an Old English style, Main Street or Front Street was renamed Downing Street. Today, the Downing Street area is in the National Register of Historic Places, and the depot serves as a community center.

"BIRDSEYE VIEW," HOLLISTER. Several early landmarks are visible in this photograph. Turkey Creek is on the far left. Ye English Inn is in the center of the image, featuring its rock and timber design. Directly across the train tracks from the inn is the railroad station. The two prominent roofs up the hill are the Log Cabin Hotel and the Presbyterian church.

YE ENGLISH INN. The hotel in Hollister opened in 1913 and anchored one end of the business district. The original building was smaller, but renovations throughout the years have added a story. A major renovation took place in 2010 when romance novelist and Branson resident Janet Dailey purchased the inn, restored it, and changed the name to Ye Olde English Inn.

Y CAMP. Hollister was home to the YMCA, or "the Y," camp, located on Lake Taneycomo near the railroad bridge. The first building was constructed in 1910. Eventually, the camp included 50 cabins, a gymnasium, and a cafeteria that seated 300. This wintertime scene shows ice on the lake, an unusual occurrence. The Presbyterians also had a camp, located on Presbyterian Hill overlooking Hollister.

COON CREEK, HOLLISTER. Coon Creek flows into Lake Taneycomo on the east side of Hollister near Lake Shore Drive. This photograph from 1930 includes a "Welcome" sign while the car is getting ready to drive east up Mount Branson. A traveler headed east today would have just negotiated a roundabout providing access to Hollister or to Branson.

HOLLISTER FLOOD, 1943. Frequent flooding in Hollister was a problem until Table Rock Dam was built in 1958. In 1943, boats could be paddled down city streets. In the back with the paddle is Jim Owen, float fishing guide and mayor of Branson. The School of the Ozarks was located uphill from Hollister, so it did not flood, but students volunteered to help move belongings of Hollister residents during floods.

Seven

Into the
Second Century

As the School of the Ozarks neared its 75th anniversary, change was in the air. Dr. M. Graham Clark, the college's longtime president, retired. That began several years of administrative change that lasted until Dr. Jerry Davis was hired as president in 1988. One of the first challenges Dr. Davis faced was getting the college back on a firm financial footing as deficit spending had taken a toll.

The decision was made to change the name from School of the Ozarks to College of the Ozarks. Prior to 1987, the College of the Ozarks' name had belonged to an institution in Clarksville, Arkansas. That college changed its name in 1987, so School of the Ozarks became College of the Ozarks in 1990. The change helped eliminate any confusion about what kind of educational offerings were available as many people still thought of S of O as a high school. From 1967 until 2012, the school operated solely as a four-year college but that did change in 2012 when a lab school was established.

Under Dr. Davis's leadership, the college's finances stabilized while growth occurred in both the physical campus and the academic program. The college's reputation continued to grow as the college was recognized by a number of publications in their annual lists of college rankings. A convocation series with nationally known speakers became an annual event, and an innovative travel program garnered attention.

The Keeter Center opened in 2004. This award-winning facility features a hotel, restaurant, and conference facilities and stands at the entrance to the campus. In a nod to the college's history, the Keeter Center was designed to look like Dobyns Hall, the first building at Point Lookout.

In 2006, the college celebrated its centennial with a series of special events and a national championship for the men's basketball team. Dr. Davis's long tenure as president ended in 2022 when he left the presidency to become chancellor before retiring and being named president emeritus. Dr. Brad Johnson joined Hard Work U as the 17th president.

CLARK RETIRES. Dr. Clark, shown here with his wife, Elizabeth, retired as president in 1981 and assumed the role of president emeritus and chairman of the board. He had faced health challenges that included the loss of an eye to cancer in 1979. They spent their retirement years in a home south of campus until poor health prevented it. They sold the home to entrepreneur Johnny Morris. He developed the property into the Top of the Rock restaurant and golf course. The Clarks moved back to campus and lived in the penthouse in the Jones Building until their deaths. Elizabeth died in 1994 at the age of 87; Dr. Clark died at age 92 in 2001. Clark's retirement began a tumultuous chapter in college history. Between 1981 and 1988, there were two presidents and two interim presidents at the helm.

JERRY DAVIS. Dr. Jerry Davis became president of the college in 1988. His hiring stabilized the college's leadership and finances. His long tenure as president (serving in that role until 2022) saw the college receive many accolades. He initiated programs to develop character and patriotism, established the nursing and engineering departments, and oversaw $50 million of new construction during his presidency.

GRADUATION. Graduation is an important day in the life of any college, filled with traditions and ceremonies. Leading the way at this graduation are Dr. M. Graham Clark (first row, left) and Dr. Jerry Davis (first row, right). A typical C of O graduation includes administrators, faculty, and students in academic regalia. Guest speakers, special music, and the awarding of diplomas follow the processional.

NAME CHANGE. The School of the Ozarks became the College of the Ozarks in 1990 when the board of trustees voted to change the name. The College of the Ozarks in Clarksville, Arkansas, changed its name to University of the Ozarks in 1987 so the C of O moniker was available. Those who graduated in May 1990 were the last college graduates of the School of the Ozarks.

AGRICULTURAL COMPLEX. A significant building project in the 1990s was the Youngman Agricultural Building with associated barns and remodeling to unify the look of the agriculture campus. The "Ag Dome" provided classrooms, labs, and offices. Eventually, the second floor was repurposed as the S of O Lower School.

December 9, 1999

The world is filled with but a few extraordinary people.

These were such people.

For in their memory we shall find strength, hope, love,

And a guidepost by which to know if we have lived as well.

PLANE CRASH. One of the saddest days in C of O history was December 9, 1999, when the school's plane crashed while on approach to the campus airport. All on board were killed. They included agriculture professor Marvin Oetting and his wife, Judy, a retired Branson school teacher; graphic arts professor Jerry Watson and his wife, Pat, secretary for the C of O dean of students; aviation science professor and pilot Joe Brinell; and student pilot Bart Moore. The group was on their way home from St. Louis where Jerry Watson had received the Governor's Award for Teaching Excellence. News of the crash was announced to the campus community by President Davis at a basketball game scheduled that night. The game was canceled as the entire campus grieved. The six victims are memorialized today with a monument at the Ruth and Paul Henning State Conservation Area, the site of the crash.

NAIA Tournament. Just a few months after the tragic plane crash, a sense of hopefulness returned when the NAIA Division II Men's National Basketball Tournament was hosted at C of O for the first time. The weeklong tournament brought 32 teams from across the country to Point Lookout. The motivated Bobcats made a run at the title, including a thrilling semifinal game. They finished as runners-up to Embry-Riddle University.

Spanish Club, 1990. Since its founding, the school has encouraged students to join campus clubs and organizations. From the Square Shooters of the 1920s to the Spanish Club of the 1990s, students have found shared interests and activities in campus organizations. Honor societies recognize those who have excelled scholastically.

HOMECOMING QUEENS. The crowning of the homecoming queen has been an annual event at the school for decades. Pictured here are, from left to right, Winnie Kimata, queen in 1991; Pres. Jerry Davis; and 1992 queen Candy Gourley. It is traditional for the president to recognize Miss Congeniality while the outgoing queen crowns the new queen. Today, the queen is known as "Miss Hard Work U."

BOBCAT TRUCK. A regular part of the annual homecoming parade is the Bobcat truck, driven here by Dr. Howell Keeter. The parade features marching bands, floats, and homecoming queen candidates. All alumni are welcomed back to campus each November for a weekend of activities, a basketball game, and meetings with old friends.

KEETER CENTER. A major construction project was completed in 2004 when the Keeter Center opened. The building was designed to look like Dobyns Hall, the first building at Point Lookout. The Keeter Center houses a restaurant, hotel, conference center, and classrooms. It is located at the college entrance and is often the first stop for campus visitors.

THE GITTINGERS. Leonard and Edith Gittinger became interested in the college when they moved to the area following retirement. They took classes, helped with blood drives, and attended chapel services. Their gifts to the college have included renovations to the Jordan Music Building and the Thompson Building, now known as the Gittinger Music Building and Christian Ministries Building. They also established an endowed fund for convocations.

CENTENNIAL FRUITCAKE.
The college celebrated its centennial in 2006 and part of the celebration included baking a 101-pound fruitcake. The sheet metal shop constructed a special pan while the staff at the Fruitcake and Jelly Kitchen reengineered the recipe to account for the size. This is one of several test cakes. The final version featured the centennial logo. (Courtesy of Carolyn Crisp.)

NATIONAL CHAMPIONS. The men's basketball team, coached by Steve Shepherd, brought home a national title in 2006. Seeded No. 4, the Bobcats defeated No. 2 Huntington University from Indiana in a convincing 74-56 win. C of O's Michael Bonaparte (seventh from left) was named tournament MVP while Shepherd (far right) received Coach of the Year honors.

PEP BAND. An important part of home basketball games is the pep band. A song always in its repertoire is the school fight song, "Mighty, Mighty Bobcats." It was written by student Ronald Jay Johnson, later a prominent DJ with the name Woody P. Snow. He also wrote the song "Rocky," which earned a gold record. That gold record hangs in the college's museum.

MARGARET THATCHER. Dr. Jerry Davis and the college hosted British prime minister Margaret Thatcher as a convocation speaker on March 21, 1997. Her speech was part of a program celebrating free enterprise, and while on campus, she was especially taken with the Fruitcake and Jelly Kitchen. Prime Minister Thatcher was one of many prominent speakers brought to campus as part of an endowed convocation series.

ROY HOPPER. In 1943, high school student Roy Hopper dropped out in his senior year to join the Army in World War II. He was shipped to Europe where he was captured and sent to a brutal POW (prisoner of war) camp. He eventually escaped and found his way back to the Allied forces. In October 2000, the college awarded Hopper (center) his high school diploma, presented by Gen. Colin Powell (left).

S OF O RETURNS. In 2012, the College of the Ozarks brought back the School of the Ozarks by opening a lab school. Initially a high school, kindergarten through eighth grades were added in the following years. The new S of O features a classical Christian curriculum and operates with the same vision and mission as the college. (Courtesy of Layne Wilks.)

CHARACTER CAMP. Orientation for new students has a long history at C of O. As at most colleges, new students learn about policies and schedules. Over the last 30 years, orientation has grown from half a day to a full week known as Character Camp. New students are grouped into "families" with experienced students as "Moms" and "Pops" who facilitate a week of information and social activities.

PATRIOTIC TRAVEL. The college created a program pairing veterans with students for a trip back to the battlefields where the veterans served. One of those veterans was Col. John Clark (second from left), who served in Vietnam. Clark is pictured here at the Hanoi Hilton, where he was a POW for seven years. Students accompanying him are, from left to right, Alison Steuck, Kyle Stevens, Christina Malzner, and Kaylee Thieme. (Courtesy of Chassidy Brittain.)

PATRIOTS PARK. To pay tribute to military veterans, C of O developed Patriots Park near the college's entrance. There are monuments to World War II, Korea, Vietnam, the Gulf War, and the War on Terrorism. The Vietnam monument is Missouri's official Vietnam memorial and features the names of Missourians killed in that conflict.

BRAD JOHNSON. Dr. Brad Johnson was named the 17th president in school history, assuming that role in 2022. He is shown here at his presidential inauguration. The ceremony featured a processional of faculty and administrators, guest speakers, special music, and scripture readings. Dr. Johnson's remarks included his vision for the future of the college.

THE EMPTY CROSS™. An addition to campus in 2023 was a sculpture at the college's entrance known as The Empty Cross™. Standing 40 feet tall and made of steel, the cross was created by artist Max Greiner Jr. The idea for the cross came from President Johnson as a way to share the college's Christian commitment. Students, faculty, staff, and visitors are reminded that light passes through the cross, symbolizing that Jesus is the light of the world. The openness indicates that all are welcome at the cross. The empty cross also reminds us that although Jesus paid the ultimate price, he is alive. The installation of the sculpture also began new traditions at the college. During Character Camp, new students walk through the Gates of Opportunity and the cross, symbolizing the beginning of their college journey. Graduating students walk through the cross and out the gates as they leave C of O to share what they have learned with the world.

BIBLIOGRAPHY

Albers, Jo Stacy, and Dorothy Stacy. *Hometown Branson*. Branson, MO: Loafers Glory Publications, 2001.

Godsey, Helen, and Townsend. *Flight of the Phoenix*. Point Lookout, MO: School of the Ozarks, 1984.

Good, Robert. *Sunshine and the Bear*. n.p., 1996.

McCall, Edith. *English Village in the Ozarks*. n.p., 1969.

Reuter, Frank, ed. *In the Heart of Ozark Mountain Country*. Reeds Spring, MO: White Oak Press, 1992.

Van Buskirk, Kathleen, and Lorraine Humphrey. *Bringing Books to the Ozarks*. Branson, MO: Taneyhills Community Library, 1998.

www.cofo.edu

DISCOVER THOUSANDS OF LOCAL HISTORY BOOKS
FEATURING MILLIONS OF VINTAGE IMAGES

Arcadia Publishing, the leading local history publisher in the United States, is committed to making history accessible and meaningful through publishing books that celebrate and preserve the heritage of America's people and places.

Find more books like this at
www.arcadiapublishing.com

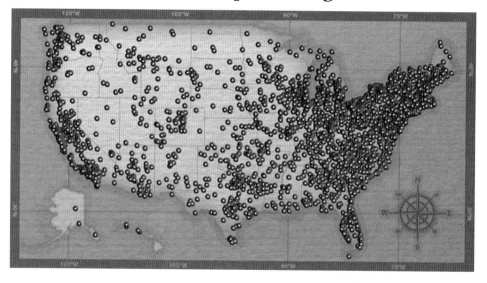

Search for your hometown history, your old stomping grounds, and even your favorite sports team.

Consistent with our mission to preserve history on a local level, this book was printed in South Carolina on American-made paper and manufactured entirely in the United States. Products carrying the accredited Forest Stewardship Council (FSC) label are printed on 100 percent FSC-certified paper.

MADE IN THE